AF413382

LULLABIES AND SINGALONGS FOR THE CREATIVE CHILD

Lullabies and Singalongs for the Creative Child

10 curiously original children's songs to share, sing, and play

Craig Faniani

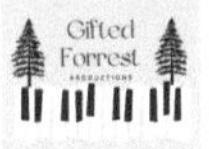

Gifted Forrest Productions

First Printing, 2024

Books may be purchased by contacting the publisher and author

Publisher: Gifted Forrest Publications

ISBN: 979-8-218-41086-5

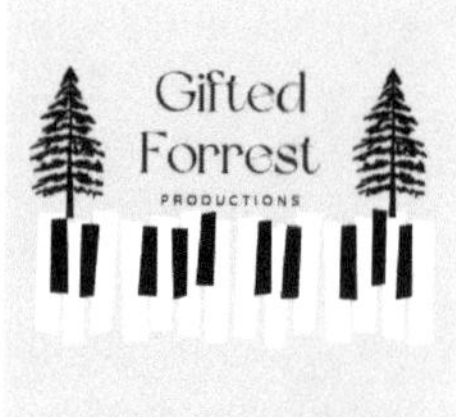

To Finley May Faniani, our first grandchild...

CONTENTS

ACKNOWLEDGMENTS

Thank you to:
My incredible illustration team- Jeff Armstrong, Judy Butler, Michael Dittmer,
Hilda Fernandez, Maryann Olés Schultz, Debbie Smith, Mark Tomassetti,
Katri Kokila Uno, Ronald Walker, and Larry Williams.
Premier vocalist, Ann Roach, on Mom's Lullaby
My wife Laurie for the encouragement, perseverance, and proofing
The newest Faniani, Finley, and her parents John and Michelle for bringing her into
this creative world
- and to my grandparents for the musical gifts bestowed in the family genes

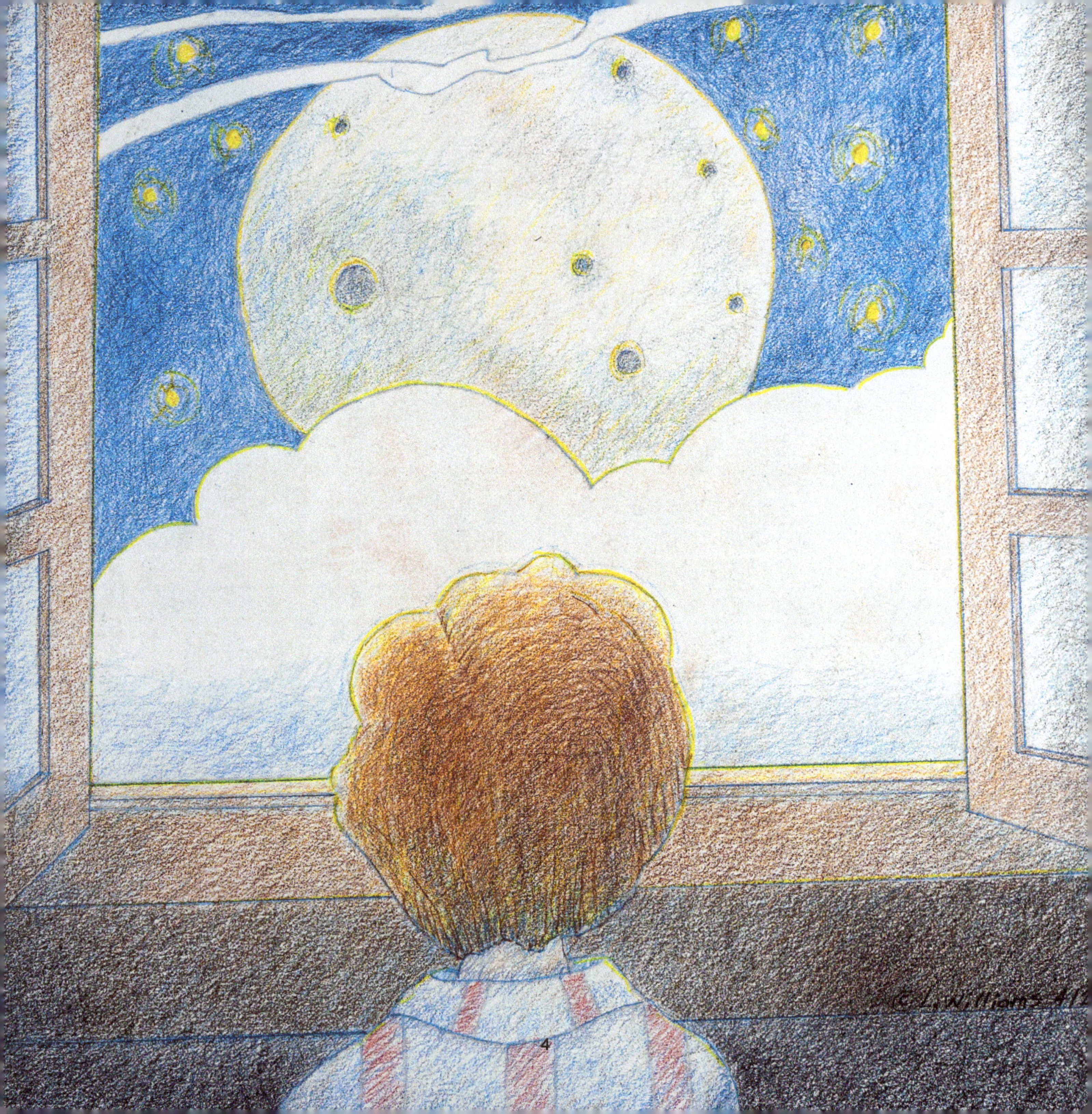
©L.Williams '11

1. DREAM LAND

It's time to go to Dream Land,
take a trip with Sandman
Never know where you'll land,
it's all a mystery
We'll go running,
skipping and a jumping
The choice is yours, the world to see,
is in your hands
Let's go see!
See over there is the Polar Express, there's Jack and the Beanstalk, the 3 Little Pigs
Cinderella, flying doggies, polka-dotted horses, think it and it's possible, imaginarily
I'll see you in your Dream Land,
hitch a ride with Sandman.
First you go to sleep,
the show starts momentarily...

Note: this is a "settle down" song - let the piano trail at the end take us to Dream Land

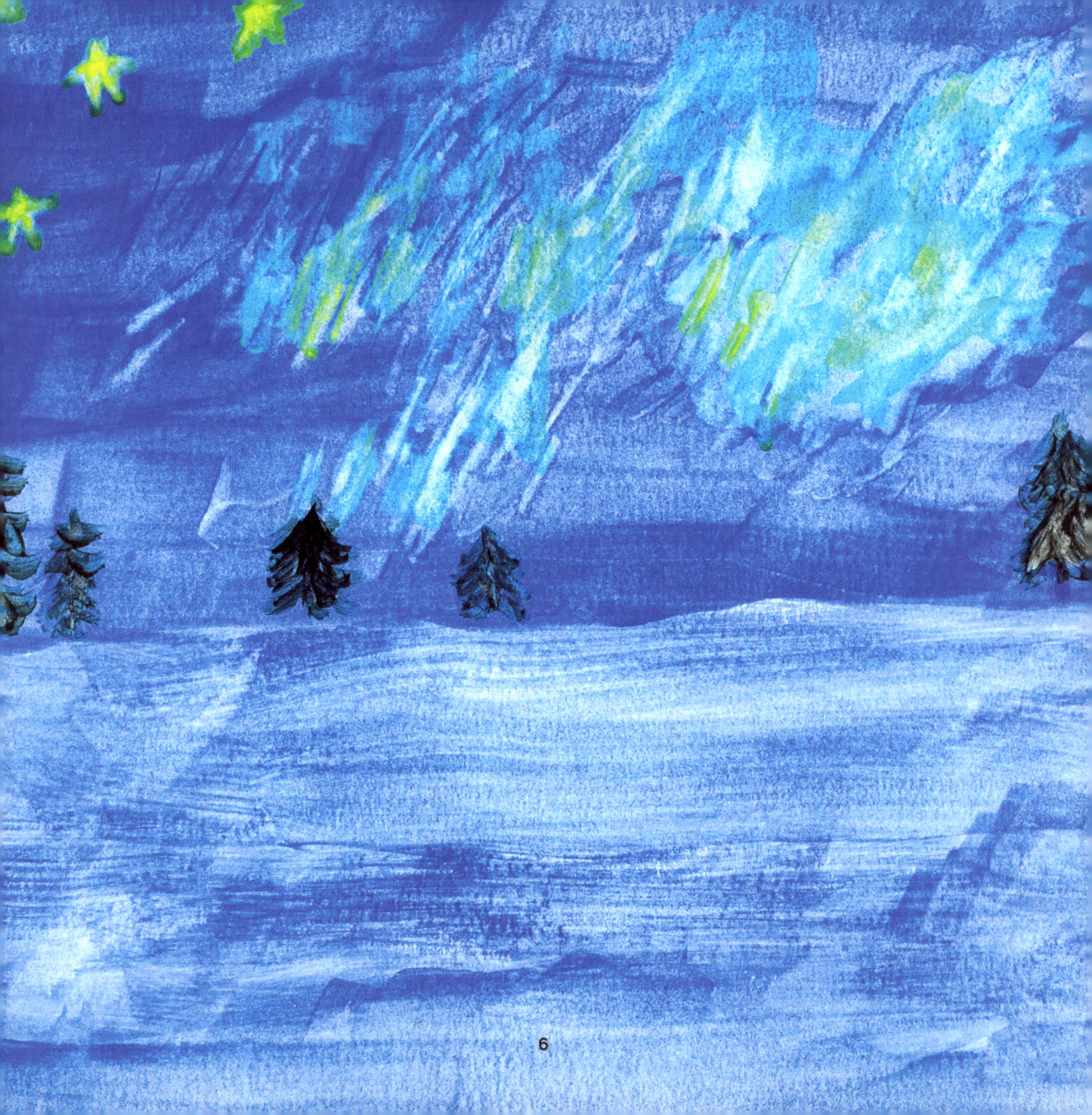

2. STAR LIGHT

Star light, star bright,
first star I see tonight

I wish I may, I wish I might,
have this wish I wish tonight

Star light, star bright,
first star I see tonight

I wish I may, I wish I might,
have this wish I wish tonight...

*Note: this lullaby starts with a piano melody, the bell tells you when to sing,
then a piano improvisation is followed by another verse*

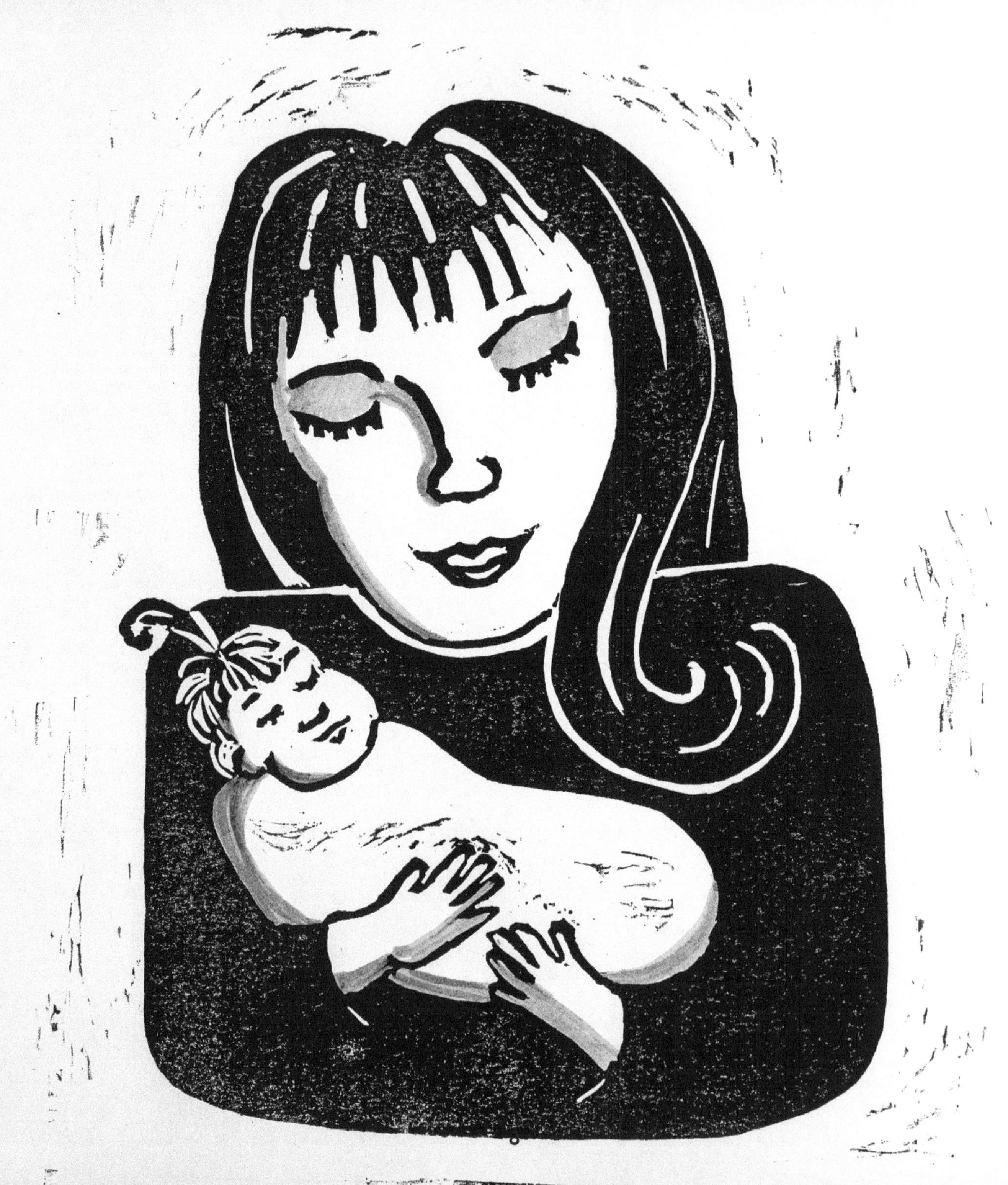

3. MOM'S LULLABY

Mom's lullaby is a beautiful song
and the melody soars as it carries along

Mom's lullaby makes you drift off to sleep
and soon you're in wonderland with never a peep

Mom's lullaby is as snug as a hug,
I feel safe, I feel warm, and I know I am loved

Mom's lullaby is my favorite song,
it will play in my heart, 'til forever is done

*Note: this lullaby is expertly sung by Ann Sabra Roach in a gentle, tender, airy style...
very relaxing and sleep inducing*

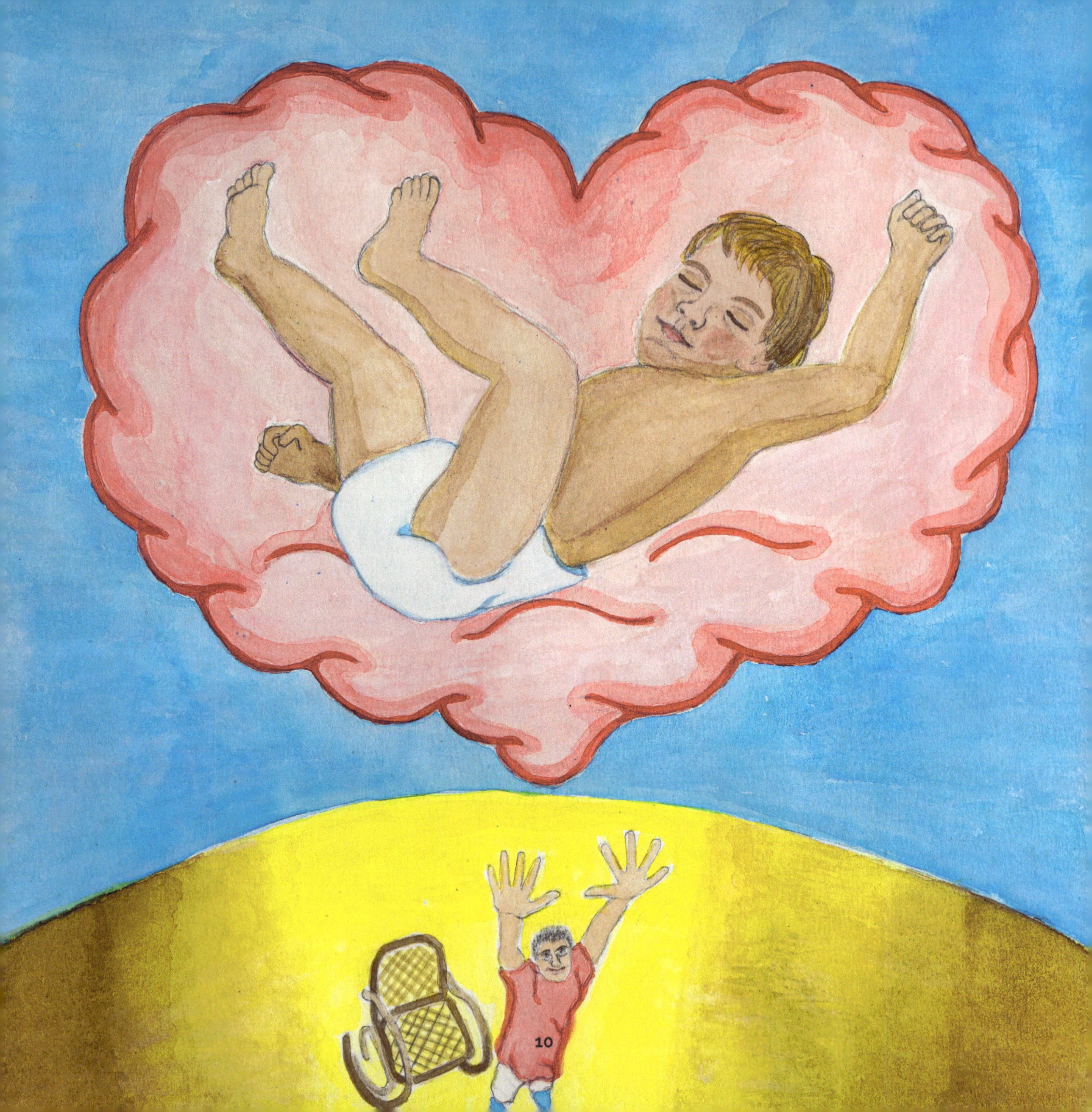

4. MY DAD KNOWS

My Dad knows how to rock me,
in the rocking chair
He knows how to throw me,
up into the air
Dad knows how to dance with me,
when the music plays
He knows how to sing to me,
in his special way
Tell me how the gingerbread man runs fast to get away
Ask if I know the Muffin Man that lives on Drury Lane
Say my feet have 5 little piggies, (I know they're just toes)
Rub my head and sing this song to make my eyelids close
I can't sing this song quite yet,
but I will someday
I can't run as fast as the muffin man,
but I will find a way
Dad says I will dance and sing,
not just right away
But, one thing that I know for sure,
he loves me everyday

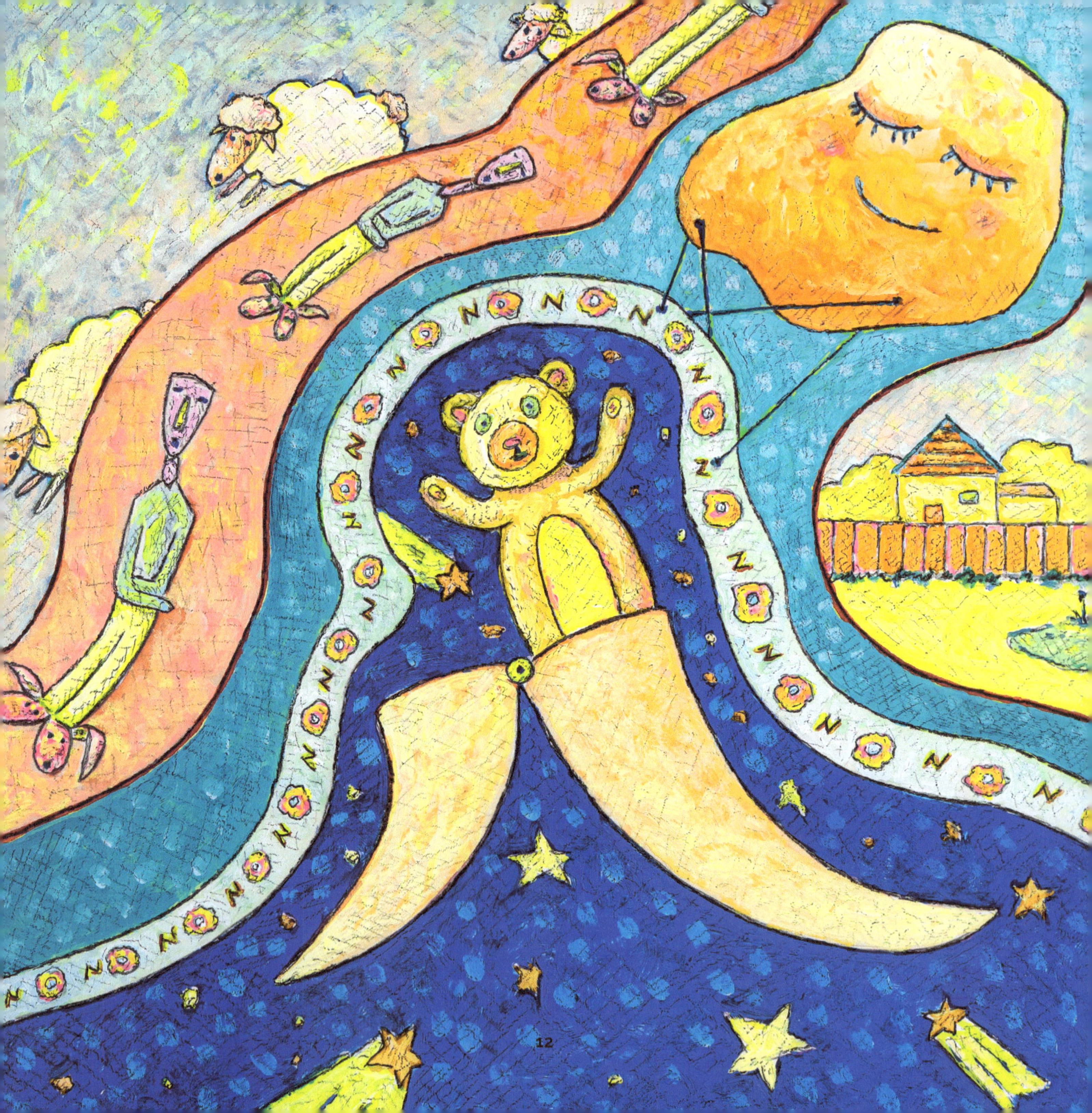

5. A SIGH IS A YAWN (WITH YOUR MOUTH CLOSED)

A yawn and a sigh are some noises we make, they're useful and helpful and we do
them ev'ryday
Let's practice to see, how they work and how they sound, so tonight,
we can use them when it's time to lay down
A yawn begins when you open your mouth, and make air noise as you breathe in
Then, with your voice starting high, let it out, it will tumble and fall to the ground
Closing your eyes on the first part will help, and slumping is good for the end
Let's give it a try - open up and breath in, now let it go out with a sound...
In..out..in..out, that's all that you have to do, in..out..in..out, sounds like it's easy for
you
A sigh is quite different, you breathe in through your nose, the mouth never opens,
but your eyes just might close
The air still comes out, with a sound just the same, but this time through your
nostrils, the sound is more tame
Let's try... the sigh... ready, mouth closed, breathe in, make a noise

In - - out - - in - - out - -
Now you're an expert with your yawn and your sigh,
but you're probably ready for sleep and good night.
Yawn - - Sigh - - (repeat and fade)

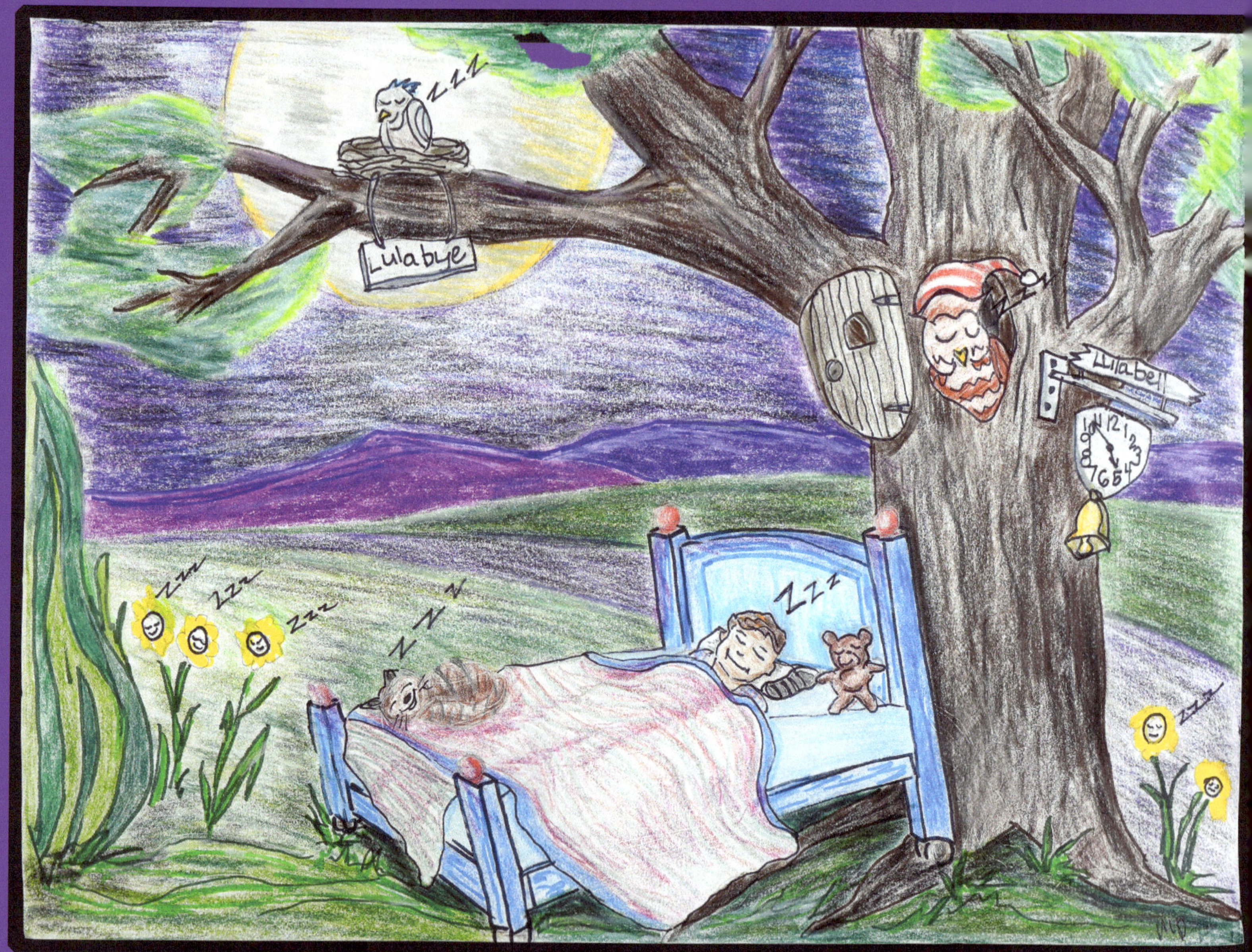

Lulabye
Lulabell

6. LULABYE AND LULABELL

I have a friend named Lulabye - She likes to sing to me
Her voice is lyrical and sweet on every melody
Problem is that when she sings my head begins to nod
Before too long I'm off to the land of snooze where ZZZs are sawed
Lulabye Lulabye I love to hear your song, Lulabye Lulabye I love to sing along
Lulabye Lulabye I'm listening right along
Lulabye Lulabye it soothes me all night long
My other friend is Lulabell - She also sings to me
Her voice is bright and loud and clear, it's strong as it can be
Ev'ry one in earshot, I'm sure they'd all agree
When Lulabell sings our ears perk up from e-lec-tri-ci-ty
Lulabell Lulabell I love to hear your song, Lulabell Lulabell I love to sing along
Lulabell Lulabell I wake up to your song
Lulabell Lulabell you're with me all day long
When I want to go to sleep, I call on Lulabye
She helps me settle down and rest, as I close my eyes
But when I want to be awake it's Lulabell I call
With 3 quick blasts her voice tells me I'm ready for it all
Lulabye and Lulabell I love to hear your song,
Lulabye and Lulabell I love to sing along
Lulabye and Lulabell I dedicate this rhyme,
Lulabye and Lulabell you're with me all the time

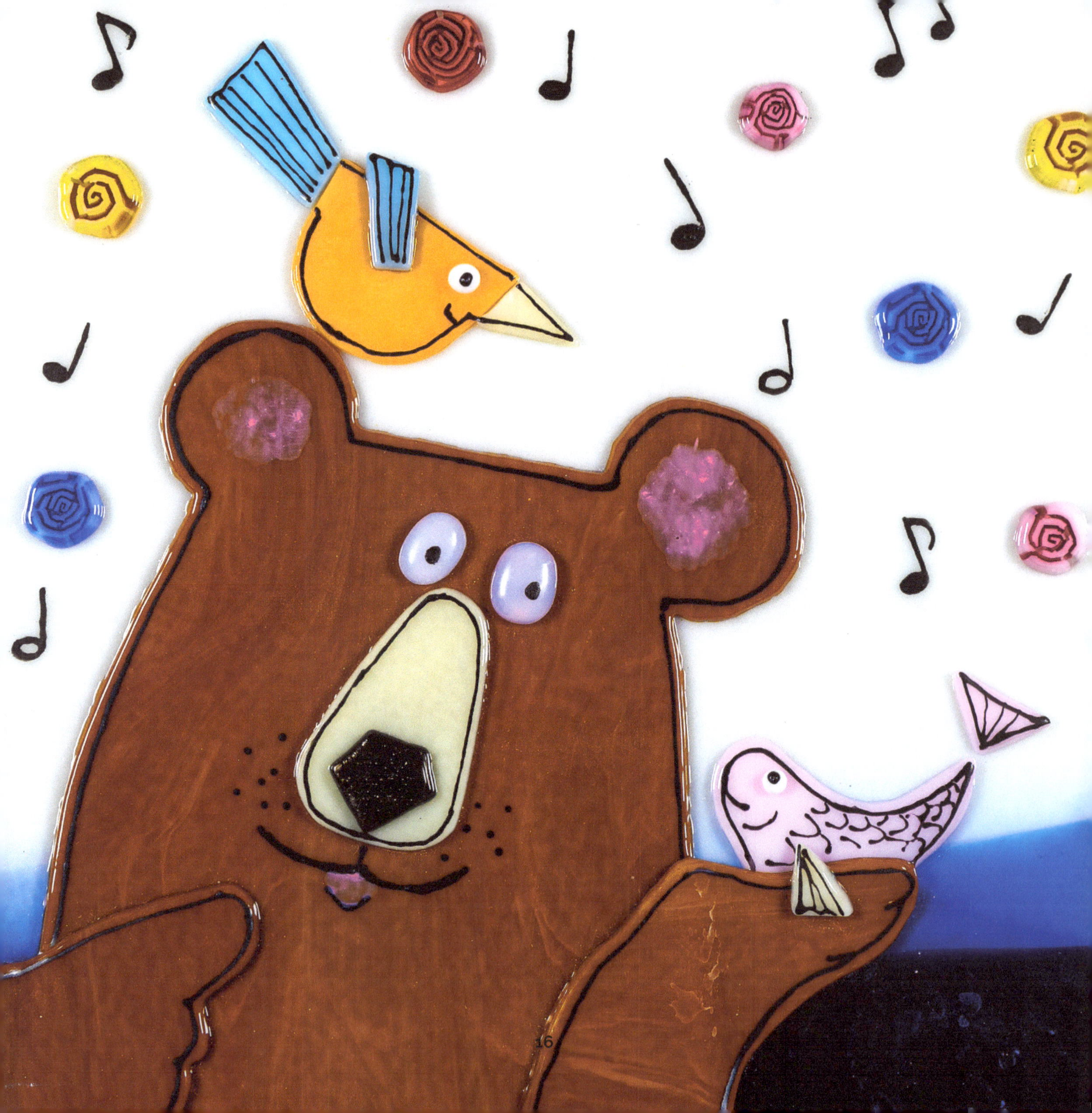

7. PENTATONIC BEAR

Pentatonic Bear sings his songs in the forest, the only problem is,
he only knows 5 notes
Then one day he heard a songbird singing, he asked her name and she said BeeCee
They put their notes together and it sounded so much better,
they liked the sound so much they wrote a song for you to sing,
LaLaLaLa etc...
They came upon a stream and a friendly fish named Scales,
He listened to their song and said there's something wrong
You're missing just one note, that will make things sound much better
He offered them a note and said it was an F
An F, he said it was an F, that's just the note we need...soooo,
They wrote a song with all their **notes**, it told their music story
The forest was alive again with melody
The bear, the bird, and Scales the fish sang happily ever after
They have all the notes they need to sing in harmony, harmony, harmony!

Note: the pentatonic (5 tones) scale in the key of C is CDEGA (tones 12356).

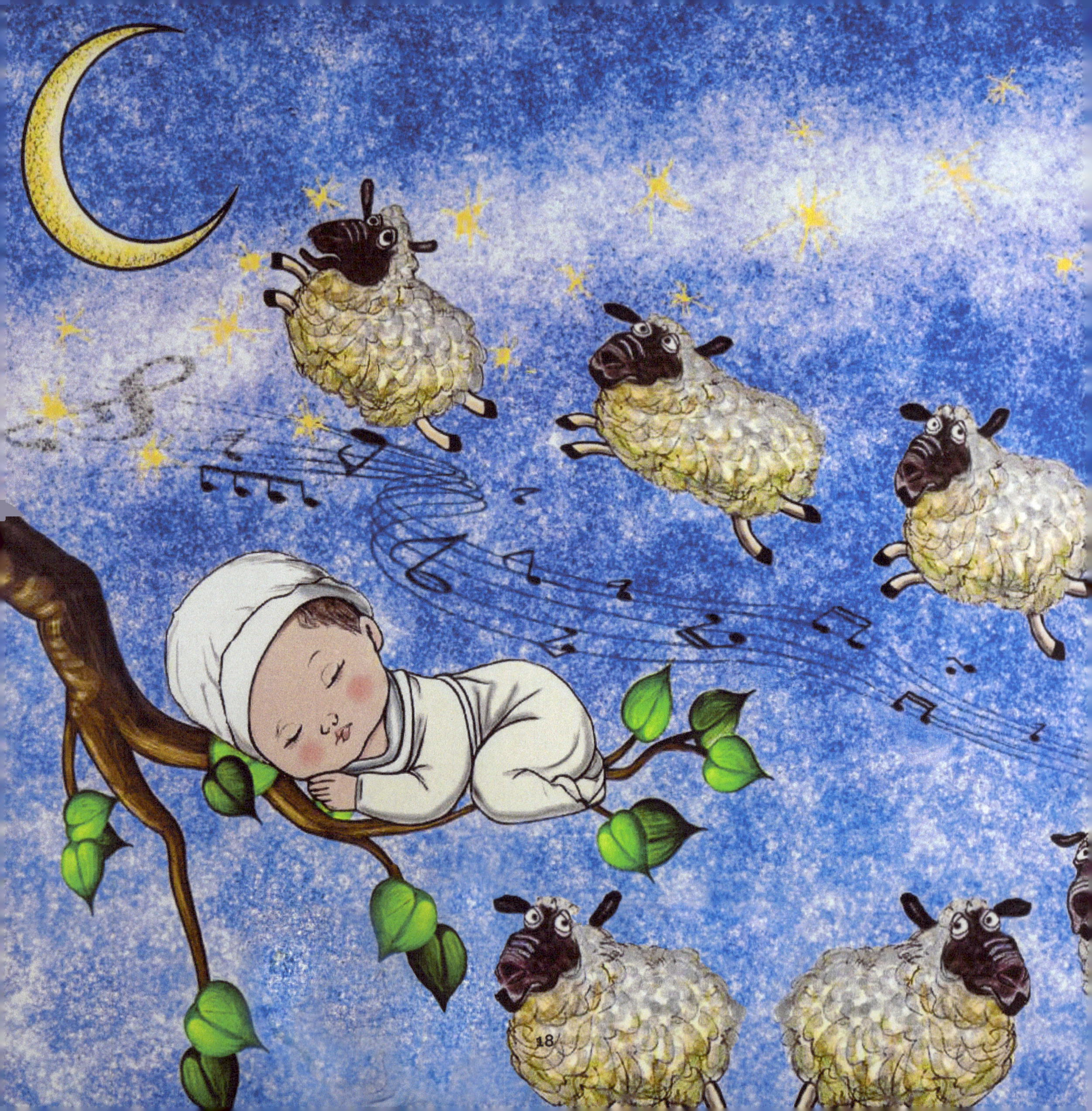

8. I'M READY

Slip slip slip slip me into my slippery slippers
Jam jam jam jam me into my jamo jammas
Wrap wrap me up in my swaddle and don't dawdle
Put my brain into my teeny weeny beanie - REPEAT
I'm a sleepy sleep machine, like it when my sheets are clean
I don't need no caffeine, I'm all out of gasoline
Slip slip slip slip…
Tomorrow is another day, I'll wake up charged and ready to play
Only one thing left to say, I'm headed for the Milky Way
Slip slip slip slip…
I'm ready for bed - ready for sleep, tired I said, nary a peep
Ready for slumber, sheep by number, my legs feel like lumber OOF!
Slip slip slip slip me into my slippery slippers
Jam jam jam jam me into my jamo jammas
Wrap wrap me, up in my swaddle and don't dawdle
Put my brain into my teeny tiny, eenie weeny, encie squency,
pepperoncini, green linguini, fettuccini, cold sashimi, beanie, AHHH…

Note: this is a get-ready-for-bed song; a pre-lullaby if you will.

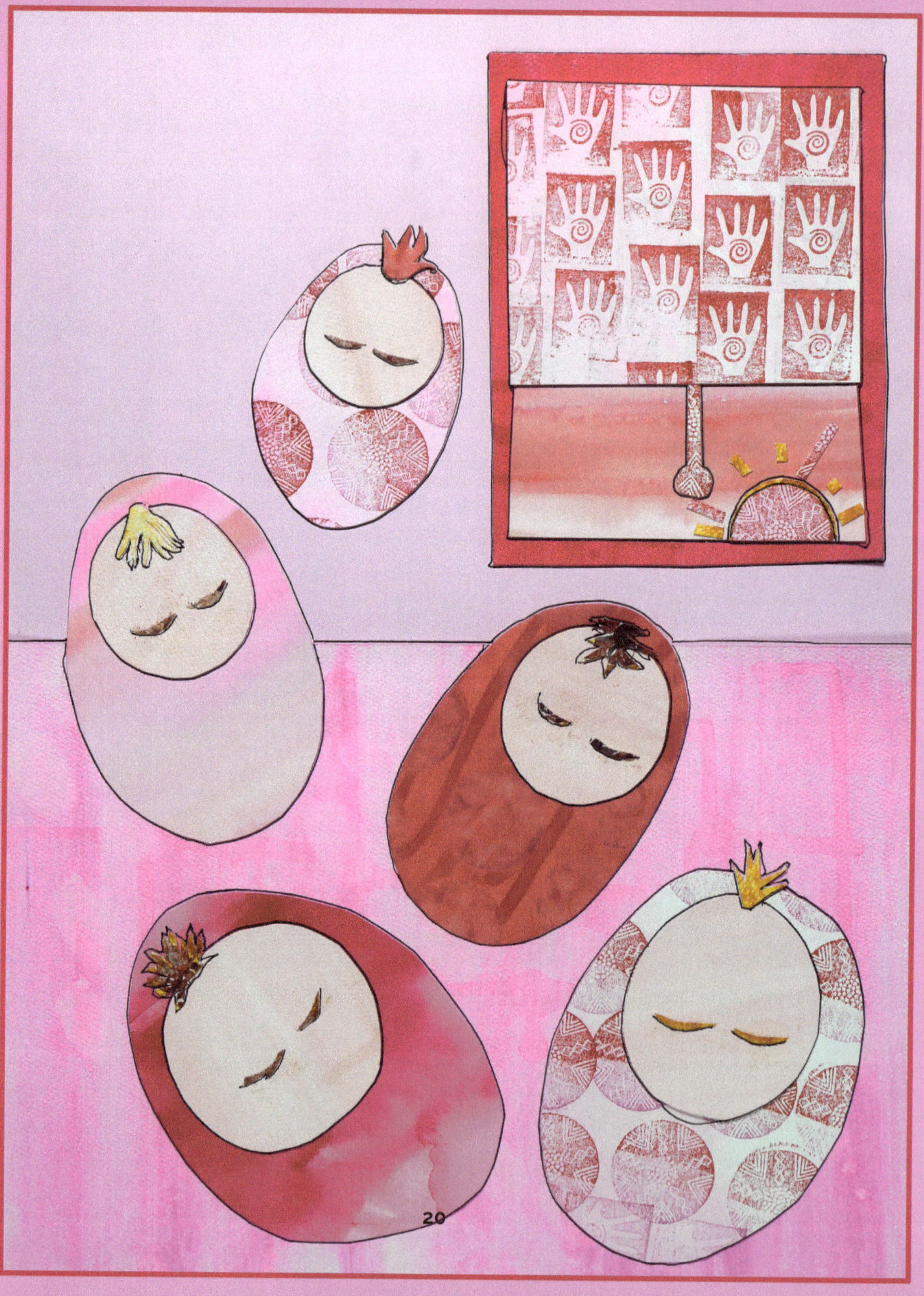

9. QUINTUPLETS

Once upon a time there was a very new mom,
she waited several months, but she managed quite a calm
Her only wish was for her newborn baby-love to thrive,
but when the day arrived, she found her total was 5
Quintuplets! Quintuplets!, you've just birthed Quintuplets
Let's not take too long to write them all their own song
A lullaby is nice, but you'll need more than just one
Or put their names together and the song will be more fun
Lula, Lola, Layla, Leila, Lyla - now that's done
But make it into a lullaby they'll fall asleep as one
Chorus: Lulabye, Lolabye, Laylabye, Leilabye, Lylabye close your eyes
Lulabye, Lolabye, Laylabye, Leilabye, Lylabye til the sun does rise
Now put on your stocking cap, time for mom to nap
My heart is full, times five indeed, the love grows exponentially
Lulabye, Lolabye, Laylabye, Leilabye, Lylabye...

Note: believe it or not, this is vowel sound learning disguised as a lullaby

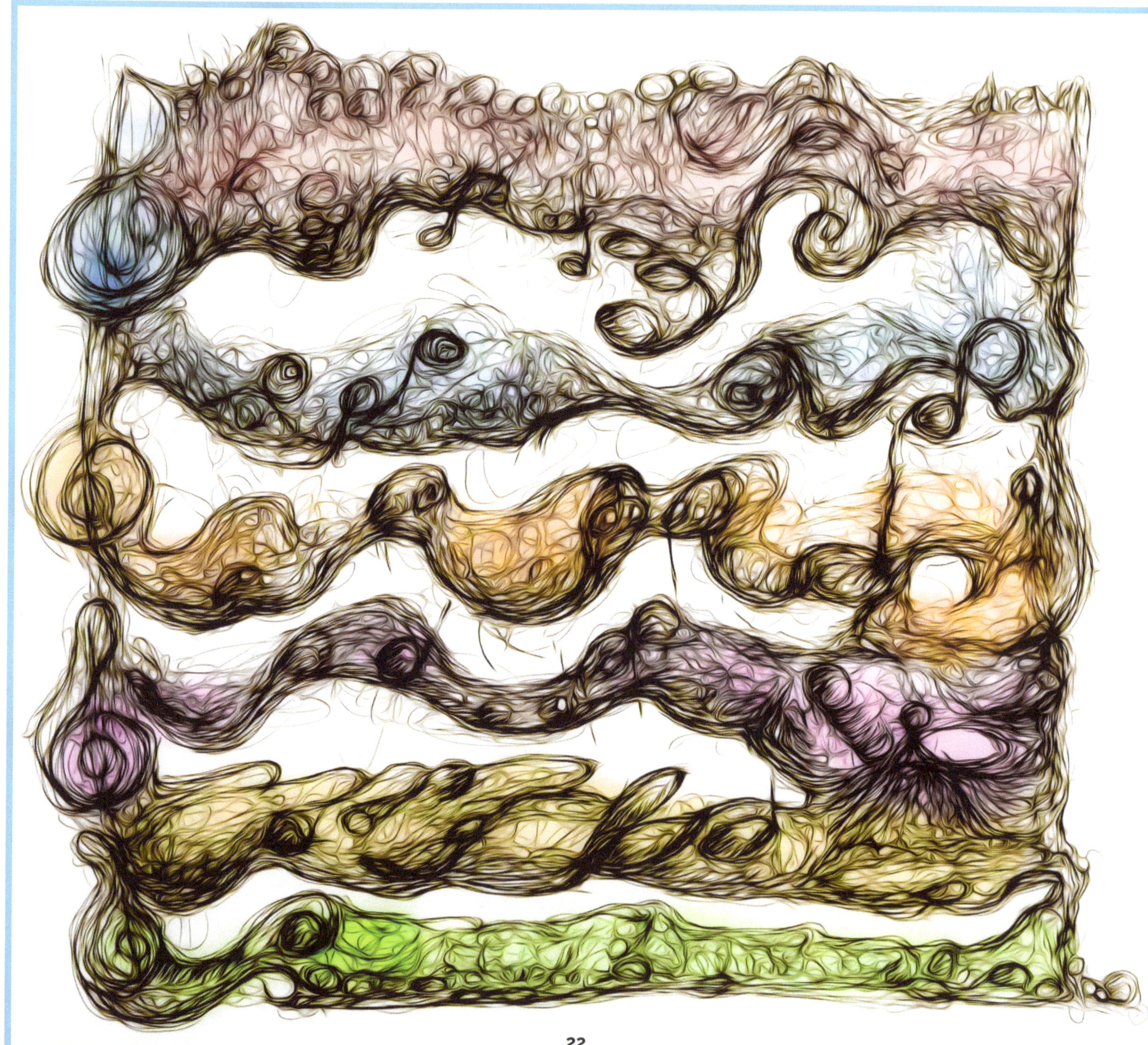

10. YAWN AND ON

Relax your toes and so it goes, the feet are next, let them know
Move on upward to your legs, they need their rest from all your play
Yawn and on and on and on, your life is but a marathon
Yawn and on and on and on, your day is now forgone
Now your bottom, it needs rest too, it's the very middle part of you
Yes, your torso needs it even more-so, take a deep breath and let them go
Yawn and on and on and on, your life is but a marathon
Yawn and on and on and on, and now your dreams fly on
Now let your arms and shoulders calm, they have been active all day long
Recline your head, it needs to sleep, off you go now into the deep
Yawn and on and on and on, your life is but a marathon
Yawn and on and on and on, you'll dance in Avalon

Note: tender lullaby centered around relaxing all parts of the body and promoting sleep

ABOUT THE AUTHOR

Craig Faniani is an experienced musician, educator, and songwriter/arranger. His passion is music, the arts, and teaching creativity to children of all ages. Craig has garnered numerous "Teacher of the Year" and "Arts Administrator of the Year" awards throughout his 35 years in education. He believes that the arts promote cognitive development, stimulate imagination, positively motivate, reduce stress, and teach joy. AND, that singing to and with children creates a loving, emotional bond while promoting language, working memory, focus, and communication. It's no wonder that his first book combines clever lyrics, catchy tunes, original illustrations, lullabies, singalongs, audio files, and sheet music. It's purposely and lovingly crafted to bring music, art, and happiness to your family...

He can be found online at http://www.giftedforrestproductions.com

Now that you have the book...

Download mp3s using this URL or scan the QR code below
https://giftedforrestproductions.com/listen-or-download-mp3-files

Download lead sheets using this URL or scan the QR code below
https://giftedforrestproductions.com/sheet-music

mp3s

the password for both pages is
giftedforrest

Feel free to contact me at:
http://www.giftedforrestproduc-
tions.com/contact

sheet music